Glynn Christian's book of ...
Kitchen Secrets

BBC-TV chef–traveller Glynn Christian has entertained on British television since 1982. As well as over 1000 live appearances, he's made series in the Eastern Mediterranean, New Zealand, Sri Lanka, California, China, Thailand and Australia. His lively, sometimes challenging, observations combined with practical fact-sharing have established him as an unchallenged authority on gourmet and delicatessen ingredients – and how to use them. Glynn's many books include *Fragile Paradise*, the only biography of his ancestor Fletcher Christian, leader of the mutiny on *Bounty* in 1789. After 10 years in Australia and New Zealand, Glynn has recently returned to live and work in London.

Glynn Christian's Book of...
Kitchen Secrets

Sizzling tips on how to cook up a
dream and achieve success on a plate

With illustrations by
Donovan Bixley

NEW
HOLLAND

First published in 2005 by New Holland Publishers (NZ) Ltd
Auckland • Sydney • London • Cape Town

www.newhollandpublishers.co.nz

218 Lake Road, Northcote, Auckland, New Zealand
14 Aquatic Drive, Frenchs Forest, NSW 2086, Australia
86–88 Edgware Road, London W2 2EA, United Kingdom
80 McKenzie Street, Cape Town 8001, South Africa

ISBN: 1 86966 101 X

Managing editor: Matt Turner
Editor: Renée Lang
Design: Nick Turzynski, redinc.
Cover image: Corbis/TRANZ

A catalogue record for this book is available from the National Library of New Zealand

10 9 8 7 6 5 4 3 2 1

Colour reproduction by Pica Digital Pte Ltd, Singapore
Printed by Times Offset (M) Sdn Bhd, Malaysia

Contents

Introduction

The best cooks just love hospitality and sharing — the sharing of food and recipes, the sharing of news or calumny, perhaps even sharing their wine if friends aren't as generous as they might be.

But none of these is a kitchen secret.

Kitchen secrets are the age-old tips and techniques that make those shared recipes work. Knowing, for instance, that root vegetables should always start cooking in cold water, muffins rise better if you put one rather than two dollops into each pan, or that you'll eat and drink less if food or drink bites back in the mouth with huge flavour. It's amazing how many cooks keep these secrets of success to themselves, even in their books. I was never allowed.

When I started cooking three mornings a week on BBC-TV's *Breakfast Time*, these tips were dubbed Glynn's Gosh Factors. I was only allowed to demonstrate recipes that included at least one Gosh Factor; so, if I cooked sweet corn fritters it was actually to tell you the longer you cook sweet corn the tougher it gets. Gosh!

Here's a collection of Gosh Factors I've collected or discovered all around the world. Weave these into your culinary repertoire, and you'll be amazed how simple secrets can make such a huge difference. You'll never cook in sizzling butter again, or be bamboozled into believing chilli is a flavour when it's only mouth trauma, not Grand Opera but only Music Hall.

So let's settle in and start sharing secrets. For instance, do you know the secrets of a decent cup of tea? Well, to start with, I'd elbow that tea cosy . . .

Seasoning and
Flavouring Secrets

Y ou've all seen television chefs do it — sprinkling and strewing with their hands held amazingly high over the bench. But they aren't showing off, rather they are using a highly practical and professional technique, because when you sprinkle salt or other seasonings from a height you are more likely to strew it evenly over the food.

—

Salt does not bring out the taste in food — it stimulates the tongue to taste the food, and thus, because we're all different, it's impossible to gauge how much salt anyone else needs. Those with dullard tongues will need more salt, while those with sprightly taste buds may need little or none. Professional chefs who do not understand how salt works, and who thus refuse to put salt on their restaurant's tables, should be run out of town. I'll be at the head of the pack.

—

Mint is one of the few herbs that tastes very much the same whether dried or fresh. Either way, mint is very fugitive when cooked, so be brave and use three times as much as you first thought appropriate. And then add some more just before you serve the dish. Did you know mint leaves are terrific in strawberry ice cream?

Mint sauce properly belongs only with mutton. So instead of serving it with lamb, bake your lamb on a thick bed of fresh mint and then, after you've removed the meat to let it rest, squeeze out the juices from the infused mint and boil these up with the pan juices. Serve as is or add to your gravy.

Professional chefs who do not understand how salt works, and who thus refuse to put salt on their restaurant's tables, should be run out of town.

When you add herbs at the start of a long cooking process, such as stewing or casseroling, all the most delicate and most delicious flavours disappear within minutes. Brighten and freshen the dish by adding more of the same herbs just before serving, ideally no more than five minutes before. One of the best seasoning tricks of all is to do this with freshly ground pepper. Heated for more than five minutes, the piperine oil of pepper begins to oxidise and develop the full but less layered flavour we are used to in cooked dishes. Heat less than five minutes and the oil will dance with savoury, herbal and spicy flavours you never suspected were there.

Go lightly with mustard when you're making home-made mayonnaise. It's not there for flavour but because it works like Dolly Levi, the marriage broker: it's one of the world's best emulsifying agents and so helps to bind the egg yolk and oil together.

Aïoli is not mayonnaise with garlic added to it; that is garlic mayonnaise — another thing altogether. Aïoli begins with at least two cloves of raw garlic per serving, crushed with a little salt into a paste. Traditionally aïoli and its many Mediterranean equivalents were made without egg yolks, but now egg yolks are stirred into the garlic paste — one or two of them per 300 ml of olive or other oil. A good aïoli should be garlic-sharp enough to make your eyes think about watering. If not, it is merely mayonnaise with pretensions.

Chilli is not so much a flavour as a mouth trauma. The culinary pleasure you *think* you get from it comes from the serotonins (natural opiates) manufactured by the brain to compensate for the pain you've caused your tongue. *That's* how addiction to the stuff comes about. Thus when you return home after a holiday in Asia and want to replicate meals you enjoyed while away, it is quite proper to use very little chilli. People who eat chilli every day from childhood become inured: in the first instance they need more and more of the drug to get any effect; and secondly their tongues become so scarred that the chilli oil has only a minor burning effect. Who in their right mind would confuse good eating with a burned mouth, and then want to do it every day?

To make a good chili con/sin carne, you must season it with a chili powder (spelt with only one 'l'), comprising a compound of spices in which cumin predominates and chilli is just another player. If you use chilli (note the double 'l') powder, i.e. just ground chillies, you add only heat — this goes some way to explaining why so many chilis are just chillies: painful, weeping, grey and pointless. You can watch *Coronation Street* for that.

Sweet Secrets

Caramelising sugar under a grill to make the crunchy top on a crème brûlée can be fraught. Instead, sprinkle the top with a very dark muscovado or molasses sugar and put the dish into the refrigerator for a couple of hours or until this has turned to liquid. It won't be crackly but deliciously rum flavoured, and neither are your porcelain ramekins cracked nor your skin peeling.

A fast way to make such a pudding without making a custard is to mix together about two parts whipped cream with one part thick yoghurt, plain or flavoured. The acid in the yoghurt thickens the cream deliciously. When it was first served to me with molasses sugar on top it was called a Dusky Virgin; pure and white inside, brown outside, you see. I'm telling you this because it took me two decades to work it out. Naïve or what?

Macerating strawberries in red wine or orange juice always sounds like a terrific idea, but it usually ends with slushy berries because their skins have started to dissolve. The secret of success lies in the macerating or marinating liquid — it must be thicker than the natural juices of the berries themselves, so the fruit juices dilute the liquid rather than the other way around. It's much better to sprinkle the strawberries with just a little sugar and then to leave them for a while until the sugar combines with the juices to make a syrup. Just before serving, add whatever other liquid you choose.

The viscous texture of most liqueurs means they can go directly onto strawberries without sugar, and then be left safely for some time before serving. You can use just about any liqueur, with the orange-flavoured ones (Cointreau or Grand Marnier) being at the top of my list. But Crème de Cacao (chocolate), Parfait d'Amour (rather vanilla-ish), Cassis (black currant), Frangelico (hazelnut), Galliano (vanilla-herbal) and white or green Crème de Menthe (mint) are every bit as good. If you use a fruit-flavoured brandy (eau-de-vie) on strawberries, you will need only a dash to taste

— but as all spirits are thin, add it at the last moment to avoid making your berries mushy, and you might also need extra sugar. I have supped deliciously on strawberries with eaux-de-vie made from *fraises de bois* (wild strawberries), from *framboises* (raspberries) and from *poires William* (pears). Peaches, apricots, nectarines, greengages, plums, white peaches . . . all these stonefruits — and others — enjoy a bit of maceration.

The traditional — and best — way to serve strawberries and cream follows the same rules. Halve the strawberries, sprinkle them with sugar, and then cover them with cream, which can be thick and liquid, or whipped only until lollopy. Leave for an hour or so at room temperature, stirring from time to time, or leave up to four hours if refrigerating. The cream, sugar and strawberry juices combine to make a wonderful pink-streaked sauce and the fruit flavour seems to double. A little rosewater, orange-flower water, geranium-flower water or jasmine essence in the cream adds a dash of aromatic magic.

Savoury Secrets

If you are making hamburgers at home, and you should, try making them the way they are supposed to be made and you might then understand why they became so popular. For a start, the buns should *always* be split, toasted and generously buttered. Yum. And there should be plenty of salad ingredients, including a slice of pickled beetroot if you are a Kiwi. A thin slice of tired gherkin, a teaspoon of sliced lettuce and a window-thin slice of tomato just won't cut it. As for the soft, steamed, sweet buns dished out by so many fast food outlets . . . only with cream and jam, please.

When you are browning mince for any reason, you should cook it for long enough that it begins to look dry and all excess moisture has been driven off and, most important, it begins to smell like beef, pork, lamb or whatever else its origins were said to have been. When you then add wine or stock or any other liquid, it will be soaked up by the relatively dry meat so its flavour penetrates to the centre of each morsel. But don't forget most mince is made from tough cuts of meat — you cannot make it tender by cooking it for just 10 minutes. Let it simmer for 40 minutes at least, or until you can crush a piece against the roof of your mouth with only your tongue.

Don't forget most mince is made from tough cuts of meat — you cannot make it tender by cooking it for just 10 minutes.

Onions that have been quickly stirred in the pan or softened for just a few minutes end up with a coarse flavour that many people actually enjoy — but only because they don't know any better. The proper flavour of cooked onion is rich and sweet, which can't be obtained after a couple of swirls in a hot pan (recommended by so many home economists, or nutritionists as we must even more extraordinarily call them). It takes 40 minutes of slow cooking for 500 g of sliced onion to change from sulphurous and acrid to sweet and delicious — only then should you turn up the heat to brown them. Do this any earlier and you are effectively charring acidic onion. And if you start every dish with under-cooked onions, everything you cook will taste the same. (Or might that be *your* best kitchen secret?) Instead, give your onions time to sweeten before browning and you then caramelise the natural sugars that have been created. Use this longer, slower technique when you're preparing a curry — or even a steak and kidney stew — and the difference will be amazing. It was done this way for centuries, until some city-dwelling nutritionists told us we are too time-poor for all that.

So if you don't have time to cook onions properly, then don't use them, or make the other ingredients work harder. If you *must* have onions in a recipe, but don't want to wait for them to cook the slow traditional way, I'll tell you a secret. Slice and microwave them, covered, but without added water until they are really soft. When you add them to the pan, they'll be sweet — and with a little gentle browning in butter or olive oil they will taste as though you have indeed put in the full time.

Raw onion is one of the few ingredients that stay on the palate —
that's why it's so easy to recognise on the breath of anyone who
has eaten it. So, don't ever serve raw onions, spring onions, green
onions, shallots or chives when you are serving good wine, or
when you plan to follow them with a dessert of any kind. Any
delicacy the wine or dessert course has will be destroyed by the
onion flavour that remains in your mouth.

Cutting Secrets

Professional chefs who care about such things can spot an amateur by the way he or she holds their knife. No, not when they're eating, and especially not if they've read *Glynn Christian's Book of Table Manners*, which reveals the secrets of doing that properly. The professional way to hold a kitchen knife to chop or peel or slice is with your thumb on top, pointing down the blade. This gives you much greater control and more power. If you hold it with your index finger on top, which most people do, the finger gets flexed backward when you exert extra power — you actually get little advantage and it can be painful.

So much effort is wasted when sharpening knives, wasted because the technique you're using is probably chipping the fine edge you think you are honing. Only the very experienced can properly sharpen a knife by holding it horizontally or thereabouts. Noisily criss-crossing the knife and sharpening steel in front of you often sharpens only the middle of the blade, and if you slap the knife too vigorously onto the steel you damage the very edge you want to sharpen. The better and far safer alternative is to hold the steel vertically, with its point on a wooden cutting board or similarly tough surface. This way you can see the knife blade is at the optimum angle for sharpening; you can also be sure you are sharpening the whole blade, from its point to the handle. Start with the blade at a 45° angle (i.e. half a right angle) to the sharpening steel. Tilt the knife in by half the remaining space, and then by half the remaining space again — this is the best sharpening angle.

●

If you must put your knife in the dishwasher it should be with the blade down if it has a separate handle, and this includes knives riveted through the tang. This way moisture is unlikely to get into the handle and then to start rot or to harbour germs.

●

Metal-handled knives can come to the rescue if you are short of something on which to stand a hot pot or saucepan. Four or more knives, placed alternately to form a square of sorts, handle to blade, blade to handle, make a terrific and stable alternative.

—

The secret to cutting evenly is to let the knife do the work. That sounds obvious, but just look around and see how many people crush what they are cutting as though they are wrestling a felon to the ground. Instead, use long strokes, back and forth, back and forth, with minimal pressure and you can then cut anything well, even very fresh bread.

—

Fresh mozzarella, the real fist-sized thing or smaller bocconcini, are too spongy and rubbery for most knives, but can be cut very successfully using an egg slicer, which won't squash them.

But a knife is not always the best thing. Fresh mozzarella, the real fist-sized thing or smaller bocconcini, are too spongy and rubbery for most knives, but can be cut very successfully using an egg slicer, which won't squash them. Another surprisingly good technique is to cut sticky cheeses, logs of goat cheese and even sponge rolls with dental floss or fine nylon fishing line. Simply slide a long length of floss or line under the food, cross the two ends over the top and then pull them in opposite directions — as you do, the floss or line will cut from bottom to top. Brilliant. Oh, it's probably best not to use minted floss. Although if the sponge roll were to be chocolate . . .

And then there are electric knives, which aren't bad but they often give a rather ragged finish to meat. Yet they are seen in many a professional kitchen — because they do some jobs better than anything else. Quite the best use of an electric knife is to cut pastry, particularly stacks of pastry as in custard squares or napoleons or large sandwiches with a top and a bottom of layered filo or puff pastry — what I call fly-away pies. Provided you use almost no pressure, an electric knife cuts through these kinds of constructions without squeezing out the fillings. They're also excellent for cutting terrines, mousses, etc. But don't press hard or you will squash the food, chip the plate, damage the table and never be asked to play again.

Outdoor Secrets

The true barbecue style of cooking — and true roasting incidentally — doesn't cook *over* a fire at all, but in front of it so drippings of fat go nowhere near the heat source. This is not difficult to achieve on a small domestic charcoal barbecue.

When barbecuing for just two or three, do it like cave men and cook the food *beside* the coals, not *over* them. Once the barbecue coals are white-hot on the outside, pile them all towards one side of the barbecue and then cook on the other side — that way no fat falls directly onto the coals.

If you are cooking for a crowd, and thus need all the grill area for food, bring the coals to a white-hot state and then put a big aluminium foil roasting tray or several smaller foil containers on the coals directly below the cooking areas. If you must have smokiness, add aromatic wood chips to the tray juices before the food is cooked through, or remove the foil pan for the last few minutes and put a package of chips (see below) directly onto the coals.

For gas-fuelled barbecues, put aluminium foil trays between the grilling racks and the gas flame, so fat doesn't drip onto the flames. Barbecues don't have to be used just for grilling. They can also provide a simple heat source, an outdoor hob if you like. Use them to keep a pot of corned beef hot, to keep a chili con carne simmering, or for a pot of water in which you heat up frankfurters or meaty garlic sausages as needed. At winter football fields, keep soup hot on a barbecue, and when the game's all over and the coals are dying, that's the time for making mulled wine or spiced ale. Make these too soon and the heat from the coals will drive off the alcohol. Red card.

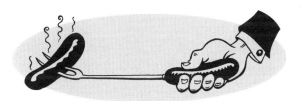

Keep sausages safely refrigerated and then precook them (see below) immediately before guests arrive, so they are still hot when they go on the barbecue. This way, there'll be no danger of them being hot on the outside and ice-cold on the inside. Precooked, the skins should not split on the barbecue and you can feel secure about not serving raw or undercooked meat. To precook, put uncooked sausages into a large saucepan with plenty of cold water and then bring them very slowly to a simmer — do not let them come to a great rolling boil. Once they've started to simmer, cook them for at least 10 minutes. To be absolutely certain your sausages will be cooked right through, choose those with coarsely chopped or minced fillings rather than a fine paste: the denseness of the fine ones requires much longer for heat to penetrate and cook.

Choose good, strong breads for a barbecue, like focaccia, ciabatta or rugged sourdoughs.

Blustery wind can cool the top of food, particularly chops, steaks and chicken legs, so one side is cold and the other burns. In such cases, place an aluminium foil tray over the meat, which will keep the heat where it should be and cause the meat to bake rather than barbecue. This method also works well for pizzas — a foil plate is perfect. But remember to punch a hole or two in the foil to allow steam to escape.

For even cooking of chicken legs or chops, or of any other cut where one end is thinner than the other, always put the thicker part towards the centre of the coals and the thinner to the outside.

Choose good, strong breads for a barbecue, like focaccia, ciabatta or rugged sourdoughs. Split or slice your loaf and barbecue cut-side down until lightly toasted and heated through. This way the bread will soak up more juices when used for open or closed sandwiches.

Hot coals need lots of air, and yet few houses have a pair of bellows at hand these days. So, here's a great way to light up the life of barbecue coals that glower rather than glow. You must ask the lady of the house if you may borrow her hair-dryer — and the gentleman of the house for a safe extension cord. Note: getting this the wrong way round can lead to revelations that are unseemly at table. Once armed with the dryer, aim a flow of air at the base of the coals and they will soon be alight. Don't comment when you see who is the more anxious for the safety of the hair-dryer.

Aromatic wood chips, especially hickory, add extra special flavour to charcoal barbecues. But if you chuck them on just as they come, they can burn rather than smoulder and there is little fragrance in the smoke.

Smoking Secrets

Aromatic wood chips, especially hickory, add extra special flavour to charcoal barbecues. But if you chuck them on just as they come, they can burn rather than smoulder and there is little fragrance in the smoke. Soak the chips in water for 20 minutes and then wrap them — two or three deep — in several layers of aluminium foil. Slash through the foil on one side, and then put the package, slashed side up, directly onto the coals. Preparing the chips this way means they smoulder and smoke longer and more aromatically before they burn, and so can be put onto the coals quite early.

While it might seem a good idea to use herbs to make smoke, that's all you're likely to make. There is only a flavour advantage if the herb contains a volatile oil — and most herbs don't. The ones to use are green rosemary branches, fresh or dried bay branches and dried fennel stalks, and these should all be placed on the coals *only* when the food is almost cooked. Dried bay branches and dried fennel stalks should be soaked in water for 20 minutes before use. Alternatively, the herbs can be wrapped in several layers of aluminium foil as described earlier. Be sure to remove them, or remove the food, before they begin to burn rather than smoke.

Saucy Secrets

All outdoor cooking benefits from muscular flavours, but this shouldn't translate into a dreary trilogy of charred meat, harsh raw onions and a furnace of chilli sauce. You might as well serve only sliced white bread for all else you will taste. Instead of including chilli in your barbecue sauce, pass around hot sauces like Tabasco, so everyone can choose the heat level they prefer.

To be intriguing as well as robust, add a very little dark chocolate or cocoa powder to a barbecue sauce that's packed with tomatoes and capsicums, garlic and cumin. They both give very good colour and add a fabulous flavour, but go carefully — one square of chocolate per serving is probably too much.

Canned baked beans react extraordinarily well to the addition of a few slugs of rugged red wine. You might also chuck in a few unpeeled cloves of garlic, some fresh bay leaves, a dash or two of Worcestershire sauce and chunks of Polish or other meaty sausage — and then leave the whole concoction simmering on the edge of the barbecue.

All those rubs marketed by chefs who have been on television more than once are, universally, a waste of money

Marinades are usually responsible for creating all that infuriating smoke at a barbecue, and 10 times out of 10 the commercial varieties will contain both oil to make smoke and something sugary that will carbonise. This also applies to all those rubs marketed by chefs who have been on television more than once. They are, universally, a waste of money, for after cooking, the ingredients of the rubs can't be tasted through the charred crust. Far better to use the natural oils found in limes, lemons or oranges, and then to use a rub (if you must) as part of a last-minute basting. These citrus oils penetrate to give wonderful flavour that adds extra zing to other flavourings and sauces, but won't drip off to create smoke. Lime is perhaps the most interesting and sophisticated choice. You can access the oil by grating or zesting your citrus of choice directly into a deep bowl — see page 44 — to ensure you capture it all. Add the meat to the bowl and toss until well coated. Leave covered, preferably at room temperature for at least 20 minutes, but if you insist on refrigeration it will take an hour-plus to come back to room temperature.

To get the best from a rub, mix it with a minimal amount of oil (or wine or lemon juice) and keep this combination warm on the back of the barbecue, which will give time for the flavours to develop. Once the meat is cooked, remove it and only then paint it with the flavourings, and then allow it to rest for five minutes on a hot plate. What might once have been burnt offerings are now heavenly tributes.

And now for the bad news: burned meat and poultry skin (including burned poultry juices) have been proven as major causes of cancer, particularly of the stomach. The occasional charred meal shouldn't hurt you, but eating charred meat or poultry several times a week is a very bad idea indeed.

But there is good news, too. If you lightly microwave meat or poultry before barbecuing or grilling it, you change the surface chemistry so it makes far fewer carcinogens if it is subsequently charred. Even so, it seems a good idea not to eat charred meat or poultry, and not to use charred or very brown juices as a sauce or to make gravy. Brown and caramelise the vegetables instead, for they do not bring the same carcinogenic risk.

Juicy Secrets

he real flavour in citrus zest lies in the oil that sprays away almost invisibly when you grate or zest the fruit. To ensure you don't lose it, always grate or zest as close as possible to the food it will flavour, so the elusive oil collects in the right place.

—

Thus don't grate citrus directly onto a wooden board because it will absorb the oil. Rather, grate into a bowl or plate. If you are doing it onto a plate, rub some of the food onto the plate to harvest the oil that is gathered there. Another way to ensure you don't miss any oil is to grate onto waxed paper; it's then very easy to scrape off all the oil and thus get maximum flavour.

—

If you are grating zest to flavour a cake, scone or biscuit mix, grate directly onto the mixture. When you have finished grating, be sure to collect the citrus oil collected inside the grater and around the grating holes — do this by rubbing on a little of the flour or other dry ingredients to absorb it and then add this back into the ingredients.

●

To get more juice from citrus fruit (any kind), roll it between your palm and a hard surface until you feel the membranes inside have collapsed. Alternatively, microwave it on High for 10 seconds or less. Too much and you will lose the fresh sharpness of the juice.

●

The real flavour in citrus zest lies in the oil that sprays away when you grate or zest the fruit.

A combination of rolling and microwave can produce more juice than you expect. So might a wooden citrus reamer or a citrus squeezer. If you *want* more juice than you expect and have neither microwave, wooden reamer nor citrus squeezer, improvise with the end of a single beater from an electric beater — push it into the flesh of a cut lemon, orange, etc. as you turn it back and forth. Always assuming you have an electric beater . . . .

Pouring the squeezed juice through a strainer gets rid of unwanted pulp and pips. If you have no strainer, check your hands for cuts and abrasions (it can be quite painful otherwise) and having given yourself an all-clear, you can strain out the pips by pouring the juice onto your upturned fingers and then letting it dribble through. You know, the way Jamie does for every recipe.

Add a few drops of lemon juice to orange juice whenever you are using it: this makes the orange flavour more intense.

Pour orange or grapefruit juice over muesli rather than milk. Citrus juices release iron that otherwise cannot be absorbed by the body. It tastes great, too. Porridge eaters can drink juice or eat the fruit. Do neither if you are male and middle-aged — or older. A high iron intake is then a bad thing. What is middle-aged? Well, 70–75 if you are male; 40–45 if you are a female partner; and anything over 29 if you ask your son or daughter.

You can strain out the pips by pouring the juice onto your upturned fingers and then letting it dribble through. You know, the way Jamie does for every recipe.

Zesty Secrets

Dried tangerine, mandarin, sweet orange and other citrus zests are common flavourings for meat dishes in places as far apart as Provence and China. Slice away as much as you can of the white from inside the skin. Cut the remaining skin into very thin strips, as long or as short as you like, and then arrange them around the edge of a microwave-safe plate. Microwave for two minutes on High and thereafter in bursts of 30 seconds, rearranging the strips for even drying after each burst. They can take five or more minutes to dry. When dried and cooled, store them in a jar out of the light. They will darken and increase in flavour over many years. Use in small amounts for any meat stew, especially richer or fattier stews, like oxtail. They are good finely chopped into salad dressings, too. If this is all too much for you, look out for bottles of cold-pressed lime, lemon or orange oil. They last forever and give an absolutely clear, direct and accurate flavour; perfectly ambrosial if you flavour olive oil with a few drops and then toss into cooked, warm pasta.

kitchen
secrets

Poultry
Secrets

The practice of trussing poultry goes back to the days of spit-roasting, when birds had to be evenly shaped in order to accommodate the even turn of the spit. Today it's just a way butchers and supermarkets have of making them look neat and tidy — and neatness and tidiness often indicate someone more interested in appearances than in flavour. Give me an untidy cook and a tasty meal, every time.

Trussing also prevents heat reaching the densest part of the bird and so the breast tends to get overcooked and to dry out while the rest is still cooking. This didn't matter when a bird was turning on a spit as all the juices stayed inside and the breast was always juicy.

The most extended laughter and applause I ever had from a live television audience came about when I told them a bird should rarely be seen on her back. It was in Sydney, Australia, so you can imagine what they thought I meant. And then I told them splayed legs are ideal . . .

Neatness and tidiness often indicate someone more interested in appearances than in flavour. Give me an untidy cook and a tasty meal, every time.

To prepare a bird of any kind for roasting, first cut away any trussing and then gently pull the legs away from the body without breaking the skin. Cook the bird on one side and then on the other. About 10–20 minutes before the cooking time is up, turn the bird on its back and carefully cut the loose skin between the leg and the carcass to reveal the inner leg joint; this should look pink. If it has cooked through, you waited too long to do this. Still on its back and with the legs pulled well away from the carcass, return the bird to the oven to finish the cooking; it will be finished when the inner joint no longer looks pink and the juices will run clear. Remove the bird from the oven, turn it onto its breast and let it rest for at least 10 minutes before carving (more about this shortly). Allow a turkey to rest for at least 30 minutes — it will still be piping hot.

Did you know the word 'roasting' properly means to cook in front of a fire? Technically speaking, what most of us do when we cook a bird in the oven is to bake it. Curiously, it is Americans who most often get the terminology right.

—

If you fear turning a bird onto its chest will compress the flesh, act like a gentleman on its behalf and arrange for it to take the weight on its 'elbows', i.e. balance a raw potato or such under each wing so the breast is not under pressure.

—

To prepare a bird of any kind for roasting, first cut away any trussing and then gently pull the legs away from the body without breaking the skin.

In many countries a small chicken is known as a spatchcock, but the term actually refers to the method of cooking a bird flat. It can be done with any bird, and while it does not require the discovery of roadkill, the bird should definitely be dead. This method can save 50% of the usual cooking time. Cut along both sides of the backbone of the bird and then discard this. Lay the bird skin-side up on a firm surface, and then, using the heel of your hand to press firmly on the front of the breast, keep pressing until you hear the wishbone break. Season lightly, and cook skin-side down, turning the bird skin-side up for the last 10 minutes of the cooking time. Remember to invert again when you take it out of the oven to rest before carving it.

Any bird can be spatchcocked, e.g. a spatchcocked turkey cooked in a covered barbecue makes Christmas dinner very much faster and juicier.

Game birds such as pheasant, grouse and wild duck have almost no fat under their skin so plucking them to preserve the skin does little to help to keep the breast moist during roasting. It's smarter and faster to avoid plucking altogether and simply to skin them, feathers and all. Slice through the skin along the back and then peel the skin off. Use rather more butter, bacon or olive oil when cooking them.

●

Whatever way you roast, bake, spatchcock or barbecue a bird, it must rest after being removed from the heat before you cut it, for then the juices that have been attracted to the surface go back to where they belong, the muscles relax, and you have a tender, juicy bird.

●

Carving Secrets

Nervous carvers will more calmly face the family table if they perform the following operation on a bird before it is cooked. Turn the remaining neck skin back over the breast, and then use a small, very sharp knife to excavate the wishbone. With this little bone removed, carving is a doddle.

When you are serving large numbers, it is faster to remove each side of the cooked breast in one piece. Cut inside the bone that runs the length of the chest side of the bird until you reach the ribcage. Then cut the breast away, following the shape of the ribcage until you reach the leg joint. Place the first side on a warm plate while you remove the second side. While you are thus occupied, get someone else to slice the first liberated breast as though it were a loaf of bread, on an angle for the best look.

Accessories

A metal rack or cradle, which suspends poultry upside down over a roasting pan, is a very good thing as it keeps the juices in the breast. There seems also to be a big following for cooking the bird upright, supported by something wedged into its bottom. Beer or soft drink cans are highly recommended for this purpose, but opinions diverge as to whether the can should contain some of its original content. An old jam jar minus its lid will do the trick, too. Whatever your preference, the can must, in any case, be open. Those of more delicate sensibilities might resort to using the centre portion of a glass or metal ring or tube cake mould, which has the added advantage of collecting juices in the circle intended for a cake mix.

Stir-fry Secrets

In the lands of real wok cookery, the flames of an open fire or of forced-air gas flames lick up the sides of a wok. Without these long flames you can never get the proper heat, the wok is unevenly heated anyway, and so everything stews rather than stir-fries.

●

Frankly, most wok cookery in Western countries is a waste of time unless you are cooking very few ingredients. The moment you have more than a few ingredients in the wok you are likely to stew them, rather than wok-cooking them. Thus it's as well — if not better — to use a flat-bottomed wok, or even your big old frying pan, to gain maximum direct surface heat.

●

If you want to use a wok to cook for three or more, the food should be largely precooked before it is added. Otherwise you will find the sheer quantity involved will reduce the heat of the other ingredients and of the wok, will stew the ingredients in steamy juices and won't cook them enough.

—

Ingredients for wok cookery should be cut up to have broadly similar weights. Light, moist vegetables (e.g. zucchini) can thus be cut to be twice as big as dense ones such as carrots. Lightly precooking stir-fry vegetables in the microwave means they will be evenly hot through and evenly cooked. Then add them to the wok just to finish and mix the dish. Do the same with any seafood you might add towards the end of a stir-frying recipe. This technique is widely used by Asians and Orientals who live in the West.

—

Unlike frying pans, woks should always be heated until smoking *before* you add oil or food; this helps build up a non-stick surface. To preserve a carefully developed non-stick surface, woks should be rinsed quickly while still hot, without the use of any detergent or soap, and then wiped dry.

If you add liquid directly onto other stir-fry ingredients in a wok, it will reduce the temperature and risk the food going mushy. Avoid this by pouring the liquid around the top edge of the wok and letting it run down into the base into the ingredients — by the time it reaches the base it will be the same temperature as the other ingredients.

Healthier
Vegetable Secrets

There should be no secrets about the best way to cook vegetables. In order of maximum nutritional benefit, this is by:

> *microwaving*
> *steaming in bamboo*
> *stir-frying*
> *steaming in metal*
> *boiling*

Yep, you read it right — steaming vegetables the way we do in our Western culture is only marginally better than boiling them.

But first, a word or two about the vegetables themselves. Whatever way you cook them, frozen vegetables are markedly more nutritious than fresh, unless the latter have come directly from your garden. This is because frozen vegetables have had their nutrition preserved quickly, often within hours of being picked, which puts them well ahead of vegetables bought in a shop, whether or not organic or chilled — the longer a vegetable is out of the soil, the less nutritious it is likely to be. They might not always have the best flavour, but frozen vegetables are hard to beat for nutrition.

Whatever way you cook them, frozen vegetables are markedly more nutritious than fresh, unless the latter have come directly from your garden.

Microwaving

The best way to cook frozen vegetables is to microwave them in a covered container without added water. This results in some of their internal moisture being steamed off, actually concentrating the goodness and flavour of the vegetables. Fresh vegetables will always be better for you when cooked this way, too; only add a little water if you are cooking a large amount of root vegetables.

—

Never salt vegetables that are to be microwaved: first because their concentrated flavour when cooked often means salt is not needed; and secondly, because salt can make nasty discoloured pits in the vegetables. Salt should be added after cooking — and after tasting.

—

When preparing vegetables for cooking in the microwave, cut them as if you were going to stir-fry them (see page 61); i.e. the pieces should be cut so they each weigh about the same, allowing for texture, density and moisture content.

—

Steaming in Bamboo

In the Oriental method of steaming, the food always sits in a dish or on a plate, so nothing can drip back into the steaming liquid. More important, the steaming is done in bamboo, which absorbs the water vapour — therefore little or nothing condenses and falls onto the food to dissolve away nutrition content. Oriental-style bamboo steaming comes a close second to microwaving for optimum health benefits.

Stir-frying

Stir-frying vegetables is the next healthiest way to cook them, because they usually do not come into contact with any liquid and so there is nothing to extract or dilute their goodness. But if there is liquid in the stir-fry, it is usually served with the vegetables, and thus the nutrition value is retained.

●

Lightly microwaving vegetables before stir-frying them ensures they do not drop the temperature of the wok when added and therefore nothing else in the wok is compromised.

●

Steaming in Metal

Steaming vegetables the Western way, in metal saucepans, is *thought* to be one of the healthiest options but is actually little better than boiling. This method can give marginally better texture than boiling, but the nutritional benefits are among the most misunderstood and over-rated subjects in the world of cookery. If you steam vegetables in a metal container, water vapour condenses on the inside of the lid, falls back onto the vegetables, dissolves the valuable vitamins and flavour components, and drains these back into the steaming liquid. This is great if you always incorporate the steaming liquid when you serve up the vegetables, otherwise it's a waste of time, even if you use one of those French things that fans out to fit into a pan.

Boiling

Oh dear. In this method, the flavours and nutrition are largely dissolved away. But for those who *must* boil, there is a right way and a wrong way, depending on the vegetable. Anything green or delicate must be put into boiling water. Anything solid like potato and other root vegetables must be started in cold water. Following these rules will at least ensure the vegetable pieces heat through evenly at the same rate as the water and then cook evenly. If you put root vegetables into boiling water, the outside can be mushy before the inside is even warm — as everyone in the world but a few elderly relatives seems to know.

Other Methods

Roasting or grilling vegetables offers excellent nutritional value — but do it faster by first microwaving the vegetables, and then only lightly coating them with oil. Use olive oil if you want added flavour; use rice bran oil if you want no flavour but equally high health benefits.

Microwave Secrets

Microwaves work only in the presence of water and other liquids, including alcohol and fruit juices; in the presence of sugar; and in the presence of fats and oils, including butter. That is why a steamed pudding cooks wonderfully in a microwave in minutes — a steamed pudding has everything a microwave needs. Would that the rest of life were so simple.

—

It's best to think of a microwave as a steamer, something that produces wet rather than dry food. The exception to this is when you use a microwave to toast nuts and spices, which roast in their own oils without the necessity or flavour of added fats and oils. They are evenly toasted, too, all through rather than just on the outside. Arrange your raw nuts in a circle on a flat plate, microwave on High for a minute or two, mix them and then rearrange in a circle again and then continue in bursts of 30 seconds. As they begin to brown, let them settle for a few minutes before cooking again, as the stored heat will cook them a little more out of the microwave. Nothing nuttier will ever cross your lips.

—

Spices brown best in the microwave, too — it's by far the best way to roast them for a curry mixture. Arrange the whole spices in a circle and proceed as for nuts.

Microwave-roasted cumin seeds are one of the most useful things to have in your cupboard to keep on hand to add to almost any dish or as a sprinkle in sandwiches, over salads or stews of any kind. They are approaching the right degree of roasting when they smell like, well, like those fat cigarettes everyone smoked in the 1960s. Not me, of course. I was busy baking for when everyone developed the munchies.

Perhaps the best microwave spice-tip is to roast black peppercorns. Indeed make up a variety (some lightly done and some heavily roasted) to keep in the cupboard. Roasted black peppercorns will transform anything from a sandwich or bacon and eggs to pickled mackerel, a ham sandwich, or tomato salads into something absolutely superb.

Roasted black peppercorns will transform anything from a sandwich or bacon and eggs to pickled mackerel, a ham sandwich, or tomato salads into something absolutely superb.

Microwaved jacket potatoes are steamed potatoes and rather horrid, but better than potatoes cooked in foil, which are also steamed potatoes but absolutely horrid. Why did anyone ever think this was a good idea? And why was there no rising of those traumatised diners who experienced the horrendous sensation of foil coming into contact with a sensitive filling? If you *must* microwave a potato in its skin, also have the oven, well, baking hot, I suppose. After 20 minutes of baking, the micro-steamed potato becomes a proper baked potato with a crisp skin — with an hour or more added baking you get divine *over*-baked potatoes, with a robust, crackling skin several layers thick and which have developed a truly sensational savoury flavour. Frankly, these are enough reason alone to own a microwave cooker.

Incidentally, please desist from cutting a cross in the top of a baked potato and squeezing it like some monstrous carbuncle. Instead, cut it into thick slices, almost to the bottom. Pull these slightly apart and then insert fillings between the slices. Good filling ideas include alternating curls of smoked salmon with soured cream, or lumpfish roe, or caviar — with chopped fresh dill scattered over all. Even baked beans and grated cheese look a million times more appetising inserted into the interstices than when spread all over a squeezed-up excrescence. Don't do it.

Making thickened sauces, including custard, in the microwave guarantees no lumps and no burning. If you make your sauce in an ovenproof jug (three or four times bigger than the end results you expect, for it can foam up alarmingly), it can be poured directly without the need to transfer it to another container.

Gentle microwaving returns crystallised honey to its liquid state.

Forget the nonsense of putting cling film over food to be microwaved. Use a plate on a plate or a bowl, a saucer on a jug, and so on. It's so much easier. And if, for instance, you put a dinner plate over the dish in which you are micro-steaming fish or vegetables, you also get a hot plate on which to serve the food.

Putting dry plates into a microwave to heat them before serving puts the cooker at risk and is therefore not a good idea. If you must microwave plates to pre-heat them, first lightly sprinkle them with water or put damp paper napkins between them. It seems a lot of trouble.

To check if a container is suitable for microwaving, half-fill it with water and microwave it for a few minutes. If the water is at least as warm as the container, it is suitable. If the container is considerably hotter than the water, it is absorbing the microwaves and thus is not suitable.

Kitchen
Storage Secrets

Knowing where everything is, and being confident everything is ready to use, is a great way to cook. It's not something I could always claim to do — I reckon I'd miss the frantic search for something 'that should be there' but is actually where I last threw it down. But I do know how my equipment and ingredients are supposed to be treated.

Unless you have pans with baked-in surfaces (the ones you can safely scratch with a sharpened screwdriver), non-stick pans should always be hung. If you must stack non-stick pans, put a paper towel or similar between them to avoid the underside of the top pan scratching the non-stick surface and hastening its demise.

Green vegetables, salads and herbs revive and keep for ages in the refrigerator if you sprinkle them very lightly with water, put them into a plastic carrier bag, invert this and then scrunch the bottom part only, so there is still plenty of air around the ingredients inside the bag. Smaller amounts of herbs can be put into a large screw-top jar or plastic storage box and kept in the refrigerator. Don't even bother sticking fresh herbs into a jar of water. It does less than zilch.

Unless you have pans with baked-in surfaces (the ones you can safely scratch with a sharpened screwdriver), non-stick pans should always be hung.

Bread needs air around it to keep it fresh or mould spores will grow. It's the same theory as keeping windows open in old wood-built bungalows; if you don't, mould grows everywhere, usually on the shirt, trousers or suit you particularly want to wear that day. Thus a bread bin should always be very roomy. If it is small or well filled, leave the lid open or offto allow for air to circulate. Those bread bins that seal hermetically work only if there is plenty of space around the bread.

I keep my bread wrapped in a plastic carrier bag in the refrigerator. The cold inhibits mould growth just as much as a well-ventilated bread bin. When I make toast from heavy grain loaves I first microwave the slices for 5–10 seconds, so they go into the toaster piping hot and pop up brown and crisp first time. Otherwise they can be brown outside and cold inside, which means soft and sweaty and that's not toast. Indeed before electricity, when toast was often made in front of an open fire, the instructions were first to heat the slices thoroughly at some distance from the fire and only then to put them close enough to brown.

Please don't dismiss toast racks as an affectation. By allowing the slices to stand as they do, they are stopped from sweating and going soft, keeping the toast as toast. Why do people bother to make toast when they then immediately lay it flat so it sweats, and then mash it further when they butter it? Ugh. Hotels that wrap toast racks in a napkin do nothing more than perfect a way to share the smell of whatever bleach has been used on the napkin. Sure, the toast is still warm, but . . .

●

Baking Secrets

Who says people don't bake any more? Not me, but I agree they are baking less, and that is disappointing. Making cakes, pies and biscuits takes more care than other types of cookery — accuracy in measure and method is vital. Many of today's cooks don't know the baking secrets their mothers had absorbed without thinking while they, in turn, watched their mothers bake. But the results are worth all the extra trouble; perhaps this is why men seem to love baking so much. Here are some secrets you might like to know.

Dabbing and dotting butter over an uncooked dish can be very haphazard: but not if you freeze the butter and can then grate it over evenly.

So-called hot hands make it impossible to rub butter into flour; it melts, and you make a paste rather than crumbs of flour and butter. Freeze the butter first and then grate it into the flour. By the time you've rubbed it in, the butter will only just have thawed.

—

Dabbing and dotting butter over an uncooked dish can be very haphazard: but not if you freeze the butter and can then grate it over evenly.

—

If you aren't sure your baking powder is still active, drop a little hot water onto a teaspoon of it. Or stir two teaspoons of the powder into a cup of hot water. Either way should result in the powder fizzing, but note that cold water won't give a result.

—

Distributing dried fruits and nuts or chocolate chunks evenly through a cake mixture can be tricky — you always seem to end up with a layer of mixture at the bottom of the mixing bowl that's short on these extras. Solve the problem by only mixing in about three-quarters of the extras and then, as you get down towards the bottom of the mixture while putting it into the cake pan or tins, stir in the final quarter of dry ingredients.

Cutting the first slice from a pie, tart, flan, quiche — in fact, anything baked in a dish with sides — can be a nightmare. To make it a dream, fold a doubled piece of aluminium foil into a wedge shape, a little narrower than an ideal serving, and place it in the baking dish *before* adding the bottom pastry layer. Ensure the piece of foil is long enough to fold up the side of the pan and over the lip. Proceed with making and baking the pie the usual way and when the time comes to serve it, locate the outside edges of the foil and cut just outside these. Use the tab over the edge to lift the first slice.

Precooking — or blind-baking — a pastry base before you add
a wet filling is essential. If you don't, you always end up with
sticky greeny-yellow wax rather than a crisp crust. But the
fiddle of using beans or weights puts many people off taking this
essential step. It needn't be a fiddle. Simply put your beans or
weights into an ovenproof roasting or baking bag. It's much
easier to distribute the beans evenly over the uncooked pastry,
and when it's time to lift out, this is easily done and they are
then ready to be stored, still in the same roasting bag, as soon as
they have cooled.

When cutting a cake in half horizontally it is difficult to make the cut even — and if you don't put the two halves back exactly the cake can be skewed. Avoid this by making a shallow cut from top to bottom into the outside edge of the cake *before* you slice it. When it's time to replace the top, align the two cut marks.

●

For a professional shiny finish to an iced cake, aim a hair-dryer at it — the heat will melt and shine the surface, making it look very slick. You might like to practise on left-over icing first, because if you use too much heat the icing will melt and run rather than shine.

●

If you are buttering and flouring a baking tin for a chocolate cake, use cocoa powder instead of flour. You'll avoid getting smudges of white flour on the cooked cake, and you'll have heightened the flavour, too.

●

Scone mixtures should never be rolled, but patted into shape and then cut with the sharpest blade possible — blunt knives and fancy cutters smear the edges together and stop the scones rising properly. It's a good idea to preheat and flour the baking tray and then actually pat and cut the scone mixture into shape on that.

●

Muffin mixtures should be put into tins or paper cases in a single blob — adding a second spoonful of batter can make cooked muffins heavy.

●

Egg-custard mixtures, which rely on eggs and milk or cream to set a filling, should never be baked above 180°C (350°F) or the mixture will first aerate and then go rubbery. Or it will split, i.e. turn into curds and whey, and then drown the dish. Your weeping will be nothing compared to that of your quiche.

●

Egg-custard mixtures cooked at the right temperature take longer or shorter times to set according to their sugar or salt content. The higher the sugar content in the baked egg-custard mixture, the longer it will take; this is why crème caramels take forever. Conversely, the higher the salt content, the faster such mixtures cook, which is why it's so important to blind-bake the pastry base for any open savoury tart, especially quiche. If you don't, the custard will set well before the pastry is baked — who wants to choose between perfect pastry or perfect filling? Not me.

Breads baked on the oven floor can have a very thick bottom crust that can be almost impossible to cut through if you've started at the top of the loaf and sliced your way down. Avoid this happening by turning the bread onto its side, so the bottom crust is the vertical one. It's much easier to cut such thick crusts from top to bottom.

When you use aluminium foil to protect something in the oven, the shiny side should be on the inside. If the shiny side is to the outside it will reflect the heat and so extend the cooking time.

Making a tent of foil over a roasted bird or joint of meat is complete silliness. The uncut meat will stay perfectly hot for a very long time without being covered, just as it did for thousands of years before aluminium foil. Covering it with foil traps heat inside, which will then continue the cooking process. Instead of keeping your food hot and moist, covering it with foil can actually make it dry and overcooked. Then there is the problem of condensation from inside the foil dropping onto the meat and further toughening it. Curses — foiled again!

Clean, Tidy and Safe Secrets

Who would think of a rotary can-opener as a kitchen killer? It can be if you let food accumulate around the cutting mechanism, particularly if you use the same opener for the dog's dinner and then your baked beans and don't wash it between uses. Well-made can-openers of stainless steel can be put into the dishwasher after every use. But a faster way to clean them is to run a damp folded paper towel through a couple of times, followed by a dry one.

Controls of small appliances can be hell to keep clean without removing them. You can get good results by first spraying the appliance lightly with a cleaning compound and then using a softish nailbrush or even a toothbrush. Toothbrushes (recycle your used ones) are the only way to get silver or other metal polishes into — and then out of — the cracks, crevices and folds of fancy silver, brass, copper, etc.

A mixture of salt and lemon juice makes the best cleaner and polisher for the inside and outside of a copper bowl. Vinegar works, too.

—

A cutting board that might slip can be very dangerous. Stop it slipping by placing it on a damp cloth.

—

Toothbrushes (recycle your used ones) are the only way to get silver or other metal polishes into – and then out of – the cracks, crevices and folds of fancy silver, brass, copper, etc.

Short of space for preparation or for serving? Pull out a drawer, and then put a cutting board, tray or metal baking sheet over the open drawer. I wish someone had told me this one years ago!

Kitchen tongs were invented in New Zealand — they now save fingers all round the world. Here's just a few ways to use them:

- for turning meat and poultry pieces, so you don't pierce them and let out the juices, and also for vegetables that are roasting or barbecuing or grilling
- for putting things into or out of water baths, or for moving, say, ramekins when they are in the water bath and still cooking
- to move hot pots or pans on the hob
- to keep clothes moving when being dyed
- to pick fruit that's out of reach
- to reach for cans and boxes at the back of a shelf
- to handle hot hard-boiled eggs
- to scratch between your shoulders.

A tea cosy should be used only if there are no tea bags or tea leaves in the pot. Originally tea was made in one pot and, when brewed, drawn or mashed for the right amount of time, it was then poured off into another warm pot, which was kept hot and fresh-tasting by the use of a tea cosy. If you use a cosy when bags or leaves are in the pot the water doesn't cool while it is brewing as it should, and thus extra bitter tannins are extracted.

Fresh eggs will always sit on the bottom of a bowl of cold water. Eggs that are a few weeks old will begin to stand on one end and, although a bit stale, are perfectly safe to eat. An egg which floats free in cold water is very stale and possible bad.

●

The ideal fresh egg has three components when broken: the yolk, a thick cushion of white, and then a more watery substance. As an egg ages the thick part of the white slowly collapses. When you break a less than fresh egg, you get a white that is universally thin and watery. While the egg is safe to eat as long as it smells all right, it will not taste as interesting.

●

When using butter for frying, perhaps a fish fillet, perhaps an omelette, the time to add the food is when the butter stops 'complaining'. As butter heats up it splashes and splutters while any remaining water steams off. Once this has disappeared, the butter is suddenly silent, and this is a sign it is at the correct temperature for cooking without burning.

The whites of very fresh eggs do not whisk up to make successful mousses, pavlovas or meringues. If you have your own chooks, leave the eggs at least three days, unrefrigerated.

An egg which floats free in cold water is very stale and possible bad.

A final word. The parts of your kitchen that hold most secrets are labels. That's because many food manufacturers don't want you to know what you are eating. To defeat them, make the supermarket switch your secret weapon. Whenever you pick up food at a supermarket, switch sides by turning it over and read the ingredients to discover the secrets they'd like to keep from you.

For instance, most of us know ordinary sugar is called sucrose, and that there's nothing wrong with it other than eating too much of it. But did you know every other ingredient that ends in 'ose' is also a sugar? Glucose, dextrose and lactose are just a few sugars you might find trying to hide from you. And don't believe honey is any better, because honey is mainly the equivalent of sucrose broken down into these other, simpler sugars.

Fat content is genuinely being reduced, but what do manufacturers add to compensate for the lack of mouth-feel now the fat has gone? Sugar. Many fat-free products are actually higher in calories or kilojoules through added sugar than the full-fat original. Absolutely no use if you are hoping to lose weight.

Many fat-free products are actually higher in calories or kilojoules through added sugar than the full-fat original. Absolutely no use if you are hoping to lose weight.

Hydrogenated oils are another thing to think about before you eat them. Edible vegetable oils are processed to make them into a fat that is solid at normal room temperature, and these are widely used in spreads and commercial baking. Because vegetable oils have little or no cholesterol-causing saturated fat, the spreads made from them have been touted as healthy. But now we know the process creates trans-fatty acids, and tough new US laws want them out of food, because these acids actually dilute the good unsaturated oils in our body. Using butter and olive oil was always a better bet.

The greatest labelling secret of all is added flavours. If they are not a major ingredient, labelling regulations do not require them to be identified on the front label. These factory-produced flavour replacements allow a manufacturer to extend an ingredient almost to the point of tastelessness, and then to bring it back to artificial life. Or they give a taste of something better than is actually there, like adding a buttery flavour when only hydrogenated oils have been used. These added flavourings are often defended as being nature-identical, but no flavours in nature are such simple concoctions. Up to you, of course, but I never buy anything that contains added 'flavour'. When it comes to the food in our kitchens, there should be no secrets.

Index

If you enjoyed this book, then look out for …

Glynn Christian's Book of …

Table Manners

For high-flyers who don't want bad behaviour to land them in the soup